Never Found

Other books by Jesse A. Murray

Love or Baseball?

I Will Never Break

Never Found

A Poetry Collection

Jesse A. Murray

Off the Field Publishing
2021

Copyright © 2021 by Jesse A. Murray

First Paperback Edition Published 2021

All rights reserved. This book or any portion thereof may not be reproduced or used in any manner whatsoever without the express written permission of the publisher except for the use of brief quotations in a book review or scholarly journal.

First Printing: 2021

Paperback ISBN: 978-1-7751946-6-8
eBook ISBN: 978-1-7751946-7-5

Off the Field Publishing
Saskatoon, Saskatchewan, Canada

Off the Field
Publishing

Book design by Jesse A. Murray
Cover images: © Jesse A. Murray

This book is a work of fiction. Any reference to historical events, real companies, real people, or real places are used to make this completely made up story, a more believable experience for the reader. Other names, characters, places, and events are products of the author's imagination, and any resemblance to actual events or places or persons, living or dead, is entirely coincidental.

For my Grandpa Murray. My biggest fan.

Never Found

INTRODUCTION

What if? It's hard not to think about that. It's hard not to think about what if I would have released my writings back when I was much younger. After I released my first poetry collection *I Will Never Break*—14 years after some of those poems were written—I wondered why I didn't do anything with my writings back when I first wrote them. For one, I was busy trying to pursue other things. For another, I didn't know what to do with my writings. For instance, how would I get them published? Who would I send them to? Would they be rejected? But for the most part, I was afraid. I was afraid to be vulnerable and share my writings with anyone else. Turns out, this is common with writers—and anyone creative—for that matter.

It makes me a little sad to think about how my writings just sat hidden away for so long. How many more readers would my words have touched? How many more opportunities would I have to write? How much more confidence in my writing would I have had? Instead, they stayed locked away. Instead, I sit here and imagine what would have happened if I would have released my first collection when I was in my early twenties. Would it have changed my life?

Maybe it would have, but you know what, I would do it the same way all over again. I am proud of everything I have written and created, and I am happy with where I am in my life today.

The following poetry collection is from writings that were written from July 23rd, 2010 to March 6th, 2011. During this period of my life I was headed into my fifth year of university, and my first year in the College of Education. I went from a

Psychology major with the hopes of pursuing a career in law, to switching to a History major in order to get into the College of Education. With that change, in many ways I became a different person. I had no choice but to become more confident, and become a leader—you have to be in order to be a teacher. One thing that didn't change, is that I still wanted to write. And I wrote more than ever.

Just like my first poetry collection *I Will Never Break*, the poems in the following collection are displayed in sequence from when they were written, and they are unchanged.

I hope you enjoy my second poetry collection, and this short journey into this period of my life.

Jesse A. Murray
November 7th, 2020

NEVER FOUND

Take everything you said,
And throw it away.
The promises you made,
Did not make things okay.
Tear these photographs to pieces,
I don't want you to stay.
No more memories,
I've got nothing else to say.

You tore my world apart,
Only to leave me alone.
Cold in an unforgiving world,
I'm left to walk alone.
With my head down low,
My eyes are on the ground.
I'm getting far away from here,
And I hope I'm never found.

You treated me so good,
Only to treat me bad.
You took all of my dreams,
And anything else I ever had.
You stole my life,
I feel as if I'm going insane,
No more memories,
Because memories cause pain.

You tore my world apart,
Only to leave me alone.
Cold in an unforgiving world,
I'm left to walk alone.

With my head down low,
My eyes are on the ground.
I'm getting far away from here,
And I hope I'm never found.

You will never find me.
No more memories.
I won't remember you.
You might remember me.
But I will never be found.

(…Without anyone looking, I will never be found…)

WHY CAN'T YOU LOVE ME

She said,

I sacrificed,
so much for you,
I would have done anything,
for you.

But you would do nothing,
for me,
you hated,
me.

She said,

Why so angry?
Why so lost?
Why can't you love me?
What is the cost?

Why turn away?
Why break my heart?
Why can't you love me?
You're tearing me apart.

So hopeless,
I feel hurt,
I gave it my all,
only to be treated
like dirt.

Is it worth it?
It hurts.
You hate me.

For you, she said,
I sacrificed,
I would have done anything,
for you.

Why so angry?
Why so lost?
Why can't you love me?
Why can't you love me?

I love you,
she said.

FOREVER AND A DAY

I don't recognize these faces,
Strangers everywhere,
They were people I used to know,
People who used to care.
Now I see them,
And I have to turn away.
It's a different life.
It's a different day.

My past is gone,
They have moved on.
I'm trapped in yesterday,
For forever and a day.
Locked inside the past,
For forever and a day.

I don't want to leave,
Even though I am alone,
I don't want to leave the place,
That has always been my home.
Yet no one else is here,
They have moved away.
Anxious for the future,
While I live for yesterday.

My past is gone,
They have moved on,
I'm trapped in yesterday,
For forever and a day,
Locked inside the past,
For forever and a day.

MEXICO

The haze surrounding the rocks,
The clouds enveloping the mountain tops,
The moon's reflection off the water,
The sun's reflection off her face,
Now you're proud that you got her,
The moments, the nights,
All changes in the lights.
The truth, the dark,
Are equal to the smile, the heart.
Perspectives change, when the
Sun breaks from the clouds,
When the sun shines light,
Allowed to see life,
As it is and as it was,
The night, the dark,
The moon, the sun,
A Night,
A day,
As
One.

IT'S NOT RIGHT

Break apart what I've known,
I don't want to be alone,
Sometimes I want to come home,
But I don't feel welcome.
Sometimes I feel so dumb,
How did I get so lost?
Why did it cost so much?
A part of me breaks,
A part of me hates,
Only to escape,
Only to hate.
Here I am again,
Without a friend.
I wish this would end,
I can no longer pretend.
Take what I know,
And turn it into a show,
For all of you to relate,
For all of you to escape.
Watch me bleed,
Watch me succeed,
In my own misery,
In all the pain that is me,
Watch me lose it all,
Watch me fall,
For you to feel,
What you think is real,
For what I've been through,
For why I hate you,
Put me in the spotlight,
So you can emulate my life,

It's not right,
It's not right.

I AM ALIVE

I'm breaking away,
You will no longer be able to keep me,
This is all I can say,
This is how it has to be.
So don't keep looking for it,
It no longer exists,
I can tell you,
That I will no longer be missed.
My past is not here,
Only my present,
Do not fear,
I am content.
Strategy of survival,
Man I know,
It seems so trivial,
For this I show.
Take what you have learned,
Break it apart,
See my world has turned,
It changed my heart.
For the better I live,
For the better I breathe,
My words I give,
The truth I leave,
Help me move on,
For this I know,
One day I will be gone,
But still I grow.
Stuck inside,
Inside I hate,
Take my pride,

And make it work.
I know who I am,
My strength survives,
It's going according to plan,
I am alive.

ME

Living in delusions,
My life is in ruins,
I cannot contemplate,
They cannot relate,
My writings have no meaning,
My life is demeaning,
I wish I knew the way,
I wish I can change today.
Take apart tomorrow,
Drown in my sorrow,
And rebuild my life,
Take what's right,
And turn it to gold,
These dreams I HOLD,
Will only survive,
If I survive,
If I do what I love,
If that's enough,
To become,
The one,
The person I want to be,
The only me,
For what it takes,
With all these mistakes,
I have known,
I have shown,
That I will be free
Once I become,
Me.

TAKE

Take away my pain,
All my suffering,
All my life lessons,
All my gain.
What would you have,
Nothing left,
You would be glad,
With this theft.
Heartache, heartbreak,
Break apart my insides,
Take my pain, and
Take my life,
So I can feel alive.

SELF THOUGHT

Already defeated by insecurities,
I miss my opportunities,
That are right in front of me,
Lacking progress,
Only causes more stress,
It becomes an illusion,
Trapped inside a delusion.
I wish you would come for me,
Are you the one for me?
I wait patiently,
Hoping one day you will see,
Me 4 me...

(...Are you out there, waiting for me? Are you coming for me,
while, I wait for you?...)

AROUND ME

A star, the sea, the sand, a tree,
Just taking in the sights around me.
The limitless natural world,
The captivating eyes of a girl.
These are the things I can't live without,
Deep down this is what my life's all about.
The things that surround me have become my purpose,
And for once I can wake up and not feel worthless.

All my life,
What I was searching for was right in front of me,
All the things I can touch, smell, and see.
These things will be with me forever,
And they will forever hold my life together.
I will never become depressed,
I will always feel at rest.
That is what God has given me,
These natural things around me.
Enjoying all this natural beauty,
As a writer, has become my duty.

THE OPTIMISTIC PESSIMIST

One more summer filled with rain,
Just another reason for me to complain.
Some nights I feel completely alone,
And I want to run away from my home.
Not just my home but also my city,
I don't want to wake up one day at fifty,
And wonder where my life has gone,
I don't want to keep moving on,
Especially down the same path,
Meaning I don't want to repeat my past.
I no longer want to keep selling myself short,
And I know the ball is in my court,
The future is in my hands.
I can toss away my future plans,
Get out in the world and live for now,
And as if I've always known how,
To live an amazing life,
To do all the things I like.
To have a smile on my face every day,
To share my happiness and give my positivity away.
To find the positivity in a summer filled with rain,
To no longer complain,
To embrace being alone,
To finding the positive,
To live with love,
To be happy.

WITHOUT SAYING GOODBYE

I look at the clock
And it's 3am,
I'm having a sleepless night again.
I look to my left,
And I listen to her breathe,
She looks like an angel while she sleeps.
Not wanting to wake her,
I gently kiss her hand,
And get out of bed as quietly as I can.
Who knows if I was right,
I left her alone in the middle of the night.

And,
I hope one day she will understand why,
I left her that night,
Without saying goodbye.
I hope one day she will understand why,
I left her that night,
Without saying goodbye.

She looks at the clock,
And it's 4 am,
The bed is cold without him.
She puts on a robe and goes downstairs,
There is no sign of him anywhere.
She goes back to bed and lies awake.
She has no idea how long she will have to wait.
She lies there for hours and wonders why,
I left her that night,
Without saying goodbye.

And,
I hope one day she will understand why,
I left her that night,
Without saying goodbye.

Why did I leave her so coldly?
Earlier that night when we lied together,
She said,
"I want you to hold me forever."

And,
I still don't know why,
I left her that night,
Without saying goodbye.

(...I wish I would have said goodbye, I wish you would have woke up and asked me to stay, I wish you were in my arms, I wish I could feel you breathe, I wish I didn't leave. Why did I leave?...I don't know why but I feel like I have to run away, especially when things are going great. It feels like it's too good to be true,
So I need to escape. Maybe I'm afraid of things going wrong, so I run away instead of staying strong. I never give it a chance, I escape, I run away... But it doesn't make things better, it makes me regret not staying, it's a terrible price to be paying... especially each and every single time,
If I stick it through it will most likely be fine... Maybe I will stay, maybe I will come back...)

MAYBE

Maybe I will be able to hold my head up high,
For the first time.
Maybe I will be able to take up space in the world,
And people will know that I exist,
Maybe when I'm not around,
Maybe I will be missed.
Maybe I will make a difference,
Maybe people will remember me,
Look up to me, wish they were me.

Maybe I will accomplish things that many people cannot,
Maybe I will be known for my knowledge.
Maybe people will ask me for advice,
Maybe I will be a good catch.
Maybe I will be successful,
Maybe I will remain humble.

Maybe I'll write a story,
Maybe they will write a story about me,
That tells my life story.
Maybe I will make history.
Maybe I will teach others,
Maybe I will travel the world,
Maybe I will spark a change.

Maybe I will be wanted,
Maybe I will be admired,
Maybe I will be a role model.
Maybe I will be heard,
Maybe I will be a leader.

Maybe I will be immortal,
Maybe my legacy will live on.
Maybe I will be happy,
Maybe I will have it all,
Maybe I will be great,
And Maybe I won't.

TAKE MY HAND (I WILL SAVE YOUR LIFE)

You feel so alone,
You hurt yourself.
You look in the mirror,
And wish you were someone else.
Your face fades away,
The mirror breaks.
The man with no face,
Has made too many mistakes.
But it's not over,

Take my hand,
I will save your life,
Now and forever,
Everything will be alright,
Take my hand,
And come with me tonight,
I will save your life,
Take my hand.

Stand up, take my hand,
Get up from the glass,
Take the man you saw today,
And leave him in the past.
Gather the broken mirror,
And throw the shards in the trash.
I'm here to make you understand,
That mistakes,
Do not make the man,
And it's not over,

Take my hand,
I will save your life,
Now and forever,
Everything will be alright,
Take my hand,
And come with me tonight,
I will save your life,
Take my hand.

The mirror breaks,
The man with no face,
Take my hand,
Come with me tonight
I will save your life.

FORGET THE GIRL

Catch a plane,
Board a train,
Anything to get away.
See the world,
And forget the girl,
Forget the girl.

It's time to find a new life,
Admire the ocean, admire the trees,
Forget about how you walked with her,
Hand in hand in the warm summer breeze.
Look at the mountains and the rivers,
Forget when you gave her your coat when you saw her shiver.
Feel the sun, feel the rain,
Forget about all the heartbreak and all the pain.

Catch a plane,
Board a train,
Anything to get away.
See the world,
And forget the girl,
Forget the girl.

It's time to find a new home,
Somewhere new, and somewhere better,
Forget about all the photographs,
And all the letters.
Make new friends, make new memories,
Travel the world, and go see what no one else sees.
Do anything to start yourself off fresh,

And come out of this at your best.

        Catch a plane,
        Board a train,
    Anything to get away.
        See the world,
    And forget the girl,
    Forget the girl.

NO MORE

I stand outside your door,
and I am about to knock,
but something inside me tells me to stop.
I walked all the way here in the rain,
I pictured you answering the door the same.
The way you did a thousand times before today,
Kissing each other right in the doorway.
I can't believe we are not together,
I know you will be in my heart forever.

You were my life,
You are my life,
No more.
You closed the door on us,
Locked me out forever,
There is no more of us,
We can never be together
No more…No more.

We changed, you changed, I remained the same.
You will forget, I won't forget, never.
I will always remember,
things will not get better, for me.
Maybe one day I'll see.
But until then for me…
it will always be you and me.

You were my life,
You are my life
No more.
You closed the door on us,
Locked me out forever,
There is no more of us,
We can never be together
No more…No more

Even though I told myself to stop,
I knocked anyway,
I had everything I was going to say.
You never answered the door,
cause you don't live there anymore.

No more, no more, you moved away…

WHEN I WAS TEN

…I think back to when I was ten,
I remember being so happy back then,
You were my best friend,
I wonder why did it have to end?
Riding our bikes was our life,
From the moment we woke up and well into the night…

THE RIVER OF LIFE

The river stretches for miles,
I walk along its shore.
I have no idea where it's going to take me,
I just know it won't be somewhere I've been before.

After a few million miles,
I stop and rest.
I look at my reflection in the water,
When I'm alone, I am at my best.

The man who looks back at me,
Is a man who enjoys the journey.
He is not worried about a destination
Yeah, my destination does not concern me.

I can walk a million miles,
And be right where I am supposed to be,
I am always content along the way,
No matter what I happen to see.

The river stretches for miles,
And so does my life,
I walk along its shore,
All day and all night.

IT'S OVER

…It's officially over,
But I knew it couldn't last,
It's just another memory,
Just another part of my past…

MY WORDS

My words,
my words,
have you heard my words?
My story,
my thoughts,
my words,
they are the
only thing
I can create,
they are the
only thing I own,
the only
thing I am
really sure
of…

EVERYTHING FOR OTHERS

…I need to make one thing clear, not
living up to my potential is one of
the biggest things I fear…
…yet sometimes I think maybe
I shouldn't try, I don't deserve
things, sometimes I feel like I
should sacrifice everything for others…

MY BROTHER

…My childhood was dedicated to watch you win,
no matter what team, and no matter what season you were in.
No matter what sport, I was always your biggest fan,
no matter how much your team was down, I always new you can.
You were my hero…

I FEEL LIKE

…I feel like it's no longer an uphill path,
I feel like the road has evened out at last.
Finally the journey will be much easier for now on,
I no longer have to be as strong,
as stiff, I can now treat this journey as a gift.
Enjoy the moments, enjoy the things around me,
I feel like I was lost, and my own self found me.
I feel like I might even be able to smile,
and enjoy many things I haven't done in awhile.
I feel like I no longer have to run,
I feel like I can slow down and have some fun.
I feel like my life is no longer a race,
I feel like my life is starting to fall into place.
I feel like there is a destination, that I have a destiny,
I feel like out there, there are things meant for me.
I feel like I can be happy one day,
I feel like that day is not too far away.
I feel like for the first time this is my life,
I feel like everything will be alright.
I feel like I'm seeing things clear,
I feel like I have nothing else to fear.
I feel like I'm free,
I feel like me…

THE DAY THAT OUR DREAMS DIED

I still look back, I still hurt,
I wish we could have made it work.
I had dreams, we had dreams,
but the ends did not justify the means.
We gave up everything,
to do nothing?
Who knows if we were right,
I wish we were wrong,
cause I can't live with regrets,
I can never move on.

Now we'll never know,
I wish we would have tried,
I can never forget the day,
that our dreams died.
I can never forget,
I will always regret,
the day that our dreams died...

What were we afraid of?
Afraid of not being good enough?
Afraid of trying?
Afraid of dying?
Afraid of being wrong?
Afraid, afraid,
now our dreams are gone.

We'll never know
I wish we would have tried,
I can never forget the day,
that our dreams died,

I can never forget,
I will always regret,
the day that our dreams died.

ACCEPT WHO YOU ARE

…Never let anything hold you back.
Never let anything bring you down.
Always move forward and hold your head up high…

…Just stop being ridiculous, accept who you are…

NEVER BEEN

I have wanted,
but I have never felt wanted.
I have wished for,
but I have never been wished for.
I have been alone,
I have never not been alone.

I have needed,
but I have never been needed.
I have loved,
but I have never been loved.
I have searched for,
but I have never been searched for.
I have been alone,
I have never not been alone.

I have cared for,
but I have never been cared for.
I have never been,
but now I am ready…

(…I have never felt wanted, I have always been alone. But I had to go through this to be where I am today. To accomplish what I accomplished so quickly. And now I am ready…)

YOU SLIP AWAY

You slip away,
You make it easy for them to forget you.
You slip away,
Hoping they won't let you.
You slip away,
And they forget they have met you.
You slip away.

You slip away,
Hoping they will notice.
You slip away,
And it only makes you hopeless.
You slip away,
And you fade out of focus.
You slip away.

You slip away,
It becomes your biggest mistake.
You slip away,
Now it is too late.
You slip away,
And you changed your course of fate.
You slip away.

You slip away,
Only to lose her.
You slip away,
Why didn't you choose her?
You slip away,
And it's like you never knew her.
You slip away.

(...Now I understand it's me and not them who slip away, and I don't feel wanted, when I never let them know that they are wanted. It's my fault...)

THE CIRCLE

Running in circles,
Never looking back,
Always looking forward,
Remaining on track.

                                      I'm not coming back to you,
                                      But I might see you again,
                                                  Going in circles,
                                        Means there is no end.

I see you once,
I see you twice,
I'll see you again,
Does that suffice?

                                      I will never break the cycle,
                                               I like it here,
                                                   Every day,
                                               I face my fear.

You are here,
And now you're gone,
I'll be back around,
But I must move on.

                                      You're no longer around,
                                              You left at last.
                                        I must break this cycle,
                                      I must get off this path.

I'm coming for you,
No matter where you are,
I will go back,
                    I will go far.

MY THOUGHTS

…I will never lose my thoughts. The day I lose my thoughts is the day I die, but with the thoughts I have already written, I will always live on. My thoughts will always live on…

MEMORIES

Some memories cause pain,
You don't want to remember,
But they will always remain,
Nothing can make it better.

Your lost in your own mind,
It hurts more than you thought,
There is no remedy you can find,
You pray to God to make it stop.

Why is the past so bittersweet,
Sometimes it keeps you awake,
Sometimes it helps you sleep,
Sometimes it makes you hate.

And you don't want to remember,
And you don't want to forget,
Nothing can make it better,
There is nothing you really regret.

Some memories cause pain,
Because they failed to last,
But they also keep you sane,
Yet all things present become the past.

I SHOULD HAVE

I should have, but I didn't,
I thought about it, but I knew I wouldn't,
Something inside me, said,
"You know you couldn't."

Knowing I wish I could,
I know it would feel good,
But for how long,
You know it wouldn't last long.
Then things would change,
With friends it would feel strange,
But they don't know me,
Man, why can't this be?

I know it isn't right,
I must go on with my life,
Learn these lessons, lessons learned,
See how tonight my world turned.

It feels good sometimes,
Forbidden thoughts on my mind.
I know I care,
But I won't make it anywhere.

Cause my life is worthless,
I have no purpose,
I stay on my own,
Forever I walk alone.

ANGELS AND DEMONS?

I wanted to tell her,
But I fell apart,
I sacrificed my whole self,
Just to save my heart.

I was meant to be alone,
That's what I tell myself,
If I can't have her,
I can't have anyone else.

How can such an angel,
Cause so much pain,
Maybe she was not from man's ribs,
Maybe Eve was not her name.

She had once tempted,
She did change our destiny,
But I still don't understand,
How she was not meant for me.

And everywhere around the world,
They enter your life,
They change your whole world,
And they disappear into the night.

LONELY STREETS

Everybody is lost,
Just wandering the streets,
Not knowing where they are headed,
Yeah, these lost lonely streets.

The snow falls slowly,
On the empty night streets,
No one to see me there,
Yeah, these lost lonely streets.

Why don't they notice,
Those who walk alone,
Why must we make others feel,
As cold as the winter stone.

Even when we know,
Everybody is lost,
Just wandering the streets,
Not knowing where they are headed,
Yeah, these lost lonely streets.

We are all lost sometimes,
Yeah, we all wander sometimes,
On these lost lonely streets.
We are all lost sometimes,
Yeah, we all wander sometimes,
We are all lost sometimes,
On these lost lonely streets.

YOU ONCE SAID

You once said,
One day we would fade away,
One day we would become strangers.

Yeah, one day we would fade away.

You once said,
This is the way life goes,
One day we will lose each other,
One day we will choose to not be together.

Yeah, one day we will lose each other.

You once said,
One day we will just be a memory,
One day you will be taken away from me.

Yeah, one day you will just be a memory.

You once said,
One day all the dreams we had will be lost,
One day all our love for each other will be lost.
You said, our love will be lost.

You once said,
One day we will just let it happen,
One day we will let go just like I imagined.

One day it will just happen.

You once said,
One day we will miss each other forever,
One day we will wish we were back together.

You once said,
We will miss each other forever.

(...I remember the day I said that one day we would fade away, but you said you wouldn't let that happen, but eventually, we both just let that happen. Just like I said we would...)

HERE I AM

And here I am,
Exactly where you said I would be,
Feeling sorry,
For not being the person I can be.

And here I am,
You put all your faith into me,
Then you left me,
So you wouldn't have to see,
That maybe,
You could be wrong about me.

And here I am,
You were right about me,
I'm still here,
Not being the person I can be,
And here I am,
I'm nothing without you,
And here I am,
I'm nothing with me.

And here I am,
Exactly where you said I would be…

(…I must become me… I must be me…that's why I am lost…)

MY LAST BREATH

I see the reflection of the moon,
Before the current pulls me down.
I pray to God,
Hoping my feet were back on solid ground.
I don't want to leave my life behind,
I don't want to die alone,
Please God,
Bring me back home.
No more air in my lungs,
And my life begins to flash me by,
I see all the people,
Who will never get to say goodbye.
I swear even though I'm underwater,
I can feel a tear fall from my eye.
I'm slipping into the darkness,
I have never been so cold.
I will never get to have children,
I will never be able to grow old.
Please God,
There are so many things I will not get to see,
Please God,
There has to be something you can do for me.
I took my last breath,
Now I cannot breathe,
Slipping into the darkness,
Why is it my time to leave?
Please God,
I don't want to die,
I see all these faces,
And I wish I could say Goodbye.
…Goodbye…

MY SONGS

Even with no booth and no mic,
My songs will change your life,
Unspoken and unheard,
But you can recite this word for word.
Let me show you what I know,
I know your life,
Cause I have already been through it,
I already did it.
When you are just thinking to do it,
I've already seen it,
While you continue to dream it.
While you try to feel what I feel,
What I feel is real,
Now are you sad to see,
That I made your dreams,
My reality?

SECOND CHANCE

Is that alright?
Will you take me back?
I left you once,
But I was wrong,
Can I have a second chance?

I know you cried for days
I know I broke your heart.
But I want you back,
I need you back,
Even though,
I don't deserve a second chance.

(…Never lose it the first time…)

(…We need the things we lose, we need the things we give away…)

MY HATE FOR YOU

...My hate keeps me sane, even though it makes me insane, because it makes me not want to become like you, my hate for you makes me not want to become like you...and all the bad things you do. And that is why I love you...I watch you live and it teaches me what not to do. It teaches me to be strong, it teaches me not to be selfish, it teaches me not to be angry and self-absorbed. It taches me what matters, it teaches me what to care for, it teaches me what to say, it teaches me what not to say. Most of all it teaches me what not to do and what I should make sure to do more of, it teaches me to love more. And that's what my hate for you has taught me so far. For all the times I have been angry at you, I know I must go in the opposite direction. Because I never want to be hated by the ones I love. And I like to tell myself I am a better person because of it and I will become a better person because of it...And that is all I have to say...

> (...For this I hope you can forgive me, forgive my hate for you, just like I have forgiven you...)

> (...You will never know the damage done, because I have hidden it for years, and I used it to help me grow. I have learned never to let a single person bring you down. You have the power to choose how things affect you. It's all up to you...So I've learned it's all up to me...)

JUDGEMENT

I scream, because it feels like a dream,
I dream, because I have no self-esteem,
I hide, what I feel inside,
I cried, because I have never tried.

They see, only what I let them see,
They agree, with what others think of me.
They judge, when judging should be done from above,
They love, but I am never the person they are thinking of.

You hate, what others tell you to hate,
You wait, for others to tell you what's great.
You make, yet another mistake,
You break, all your ties with fate.

I become, better than everyone,
I overcome, being comfortably numb.
I live, as if I have something to give,
I forgive, those who are negative.

MISS MY PAST

Does it mean anything?
I look at old photographs,
So many memories,
But we are now on so many different paths.

I don't understand,
How we can be so close for a lifetime,
But for some reason we move on,
And I only get to see you in my mind.

I'm starting to think,
Does this life really matter,
When something is so good one day,
But then tomorrow I see it shatter?

I've never felt so much hurt,
I miss so many things,
I try to live my life,
But I don't want what the future brings.

Because if it is all lost,
What then am I here for?
I never seem to gain anything,
And I'm not better off than I was before.

So I see some people today,
And they were my life,
But they are no longer the same,
It just does not seem right,

What should we make the most of?
What should we try to keep?
I hate only having memories,
It feels like I am asleep.

It hurts so much,
That so many people are lost,
And I often get depressed,
It doesn't seem to be worth the cost.

Maybe I take it for granted,
I need to enjoy the moment,
Even though it will be gone tomorrow,
To me it has to be golden.

It hurts so much,
I want you to be around,
I want to be with you,
Especially when I am feeling down.

I no longer feel like myself,
I have changed,
This life I live,
Every day is strange.

Because I am lost,
I am trapped in the past,
Every day I miss everything,
That has failed to last.

(…I look at old photographs and honestly, they don't mean anything to me anymore, it's all over, and this is the worst feeling I have ever felt in the world…)

NOTHING TO LIVE FOR

What am I here for,
I am all alone,
Nothing matters,
When you are on your own.

Nothing to live for,
Nothing to care for,
I have no body,
So I want to become somebody,
In somebody else's life,
Because I don't want to be by myself tonight.

Take me away,
Smash the mirrors,
I hurt myself,
With all these fears.

I have nothing live for,
If I have nothing to care for.

Everybody has moved on,
All my family and friends are gone,
All I have are memories,
But they do nothing good for me,
They only bring me down,
Show me all the things that are no longer around.

And they tell me,
That I have,
Nothing to live for,
Nothing to care for,

I have nobody,
Nobody is around.

So I have to become somebody,
In somebody else's life,
Because I don't want to be by myself tonight.

Take me away,
Smash these mirrors,
I hurt myself,
With all these fears.

I have nothing to live for,
I have nothing to care for.

OBLIVION

I've been trapped in oblivion for years,
I have never been known,
But becoming known and forgotten,
Is one of my biggest fears.

I'm afraid that once they see me for me,
They might let me go,
And they will never know,
The person that I'm going to be.

But I am working hard to become great,
I just hope they notice me,
Hopefully someday,
Before it's too late.

I hope the years just don't pass me by,
While I work so hard,
To be at my best,
I just hope it's worth a try.

Sometimes all I want to do is run,
Get off this path,
Sometimes I think
That being trapped in oblivion,
Is actually freedom.

(…Maybe, just maybe, being completely unknown or completely forgotten, is freedom, is happiness, where you can just be at peace, where I am just me, where I can just be…)

(…Maybe oblivion is truth…is nirvana…or eternal bliss?…)

MY IMAGINATION

…From time to time I know that I can find you in my mind. My imagination allows me to make you my creation, it allows me to be happy for a short while, it makes me smile, but it also brings me down, knowing that you are actually not around…

I WILL BE HONEST

Maybe it is because I am so honest,
So brutally honest towards others and myself,
To the point that honesty doesn't actually help.
It can hurt others and it can bring yourself down,
I know it isn't honesty, it's the truth that I haven't found.
I do see those people who lie,
They are admired on the outside, but they are so weak inside.
Yet, they seem to have a better life than me,
But they will never be the person I would want to be.
I don't care how hard these people have tried,
I feel as if they will never be satisfied.
There will always be something missing in their life,
And they will continuously lie to themselves,
Until it feels right.
But they will constantly be wrong,
They are actually weak,
Even though they think they are strong.
One thing they do not know,
Is that to live a lie, one is unable to grow.
To be so brutally honest,
To others and to yourself,
And to look at the truth
And nothing else,
To be true in your heart and in your soul,
Is the only way a person can feel whole.

(…To be true in my heart and true in my soul, that's the only way I will feel whole…)

MODERN DAY SAINT

Does a man who sits in the darkness,
Know how to live?
Should you listen to his advice,
That he is ever so willing to give?
If he is forever alone,
Does he know how to live a life?
Does he know some sort of secret,
Could he possibly be right?
Why does he seem so miserable,
Why doesn't he listen to himself,
Why can't he follow his own advice,
The advice he gives everyone else?
Maybe he sacrifices himself,
To help others out,
Maybe he is a modern day saint,
Maybe that's what selflessness is all about.
Maybe he remains forever alone,
So he can be there,
In times when you need him,
Times when life doesn't seem fair.
Maybe you should listen to him,
That Modern Day Saint,
When he tells you,
Life is the picture you paint.

FACE YOUR FEARS

…I feel like that if you are afraid of something, when you feel like you are at the edge, once you get there, once you face your fear, you will realize that it really isn't that bad, and that edge will disappear. That edge will disappear and a perfectly paved road will appear and you will be comfortable to walk that road…

JUST ONE MORE

Well you just took—my life away
There are so many things—I wish I could say
But you are gone—and I'm alone today
I wish I would have asked—you to stay

Just one more kiss—I wish I could taste
Just one more moment—that I would not waste
Just one more time—to see your face
Just one more memory—I won't erase

Now I'm sober—no longer drunk off love
You're the only one—I've been dreaming of
Praying every night—to the God above
But I've found out—praying is not enough

Just one more night—that we could spend together
Just one more day—that we could make last forever
Just one more fantasy—we could be whoever
Just one more bond—that we could never sever

Well, you just took—my life away
There are so many things—I wish I could say
But you are gone—and I'm alone today
I wish I would have asked—you to stay.

BIGGEST HEART

I have the biggest heart,
I care for others,
All my sisters and brothers,
All the fathers and mothers,
I respect all types of people,
In a lot of ways we are equal,
We are special,
But I feel like I am inferior,
Everyone else is superior,
I look down on myself,
And they say if you don't love yourself,
No one else will.
Yeah, it will be a tough journey for me.

MIDSUMMER'S NIGHT

A midsummer's night air,
A midsummer's night rain,
A midsummer's night drought,
A midsummer's night pain.
I heard Shakespeare,
Talk about a midsummer's night dream,
But that's not what I mean.
I'm not talking about fairytales,
I'm not talk about a love spell,
This right here is real life,
And not some story to tell.
We've all heard about fairytales,
But it is all make believe.
This is written to clear the air,
This is to help you breathe.
This is a midsummer's night air,
As clear as the setting sun,
I just need you to sit and relax,
There is no more need to run.
This is your life right here,
I hope you enjoy the sight,
I hope you have learned your lesson,
On this midsummer's night.

DÉJÀ VU WHILE SEARCHING FOR YOU

It's a moment of anticipation,
And already I can't stand this situation.
I've been in many like this before,
But I wish I didn't have to be anymore.
I try to be at my best,
But each time it feels like a test.
No it doesn't seem to get easier,
I get nervous every time I see her,
I know it sounds like a cliché,
But she does take my breath away.
And time does not seem to be on my side,
It seems like my life is slipping me by.
Sometimes I wish I could have another hour,
Maybe because she is the one who holds all the power.
Since she has the power to choose,
I know I am always going to lose.
That is why they never stick around long,
And I'm left to examine what went wrong.
Then I am forced to go back out in the world,
And look for yet another girl.
Yet another moment of anticipation,
I can't stand this situation.
I wish all the searching was done,
I wish I could find the one.

A CLEAR STATE OF MIND

The tide is changing.
No. My life is changing.
No metaphors. No similes.
My life is changing.
I am changing.
I am changed, knowing
that I am going to be changed.
I'm not even worried,
I'm just going to let it happen.
No fear. But fear.
Fear, maybe because of not knowing.
No fear, because I don't really care.
I have become easy going.
Very easy going. To the point
where I don't care what I see.
Or what happens to me?
Not that I don't care,
I'm just not afraid anymore.
I will take what life gives me,
I might keep some,
I might throw some back,
but for some time,
it will be mine,
because it is *my* life.

USED TO BE ME

No stress in his life ever existed,
Everything he attempted, he was bound to be gifted.
He gave it all he got, his passion was to live,
His smiles every day was the daily gift he would give.
This was a time where every day he sailed free,
Now that little boy, that used to be me.

MR. FORGETFUL PAST

Dear Mr. Forgetful Past,
Why the hell don't you ever last?
Are you the one who likes to change?
Do you like it when I feel strange?
Is it part of the mystery that entertains you?
Do you enjoy the things you put me through?
You know, all the reminiscing
about all the things I've been missing,
what do you get out of it?

I'M NO LONGER AFRAID

I'm no longer afraid,
of anything.
I stand strong,
before anything.
I have become a man.
Yeah, I have become a man.
Responsible, looking out for others,
I have taken on a new role.
I have started a new chapter.
This is a new beginning,
starting fresh, as a new me.
Yeah, it's good to see,
I feel accomplished,
and a little astonished.
Life is good right now,
life is better,
I look forward,
and I remember.
I'm better off,
As I am now,
I am a man.

(...I know I've said this before, but right now, I feel my age...I feel accomplished, but I have so much more to accomplish...)

SO LONG

Your always on my mind,
I think about you all the time.
Yet, when I see you,
When I see you,
I have to let you go,
I have to walk away.
But I don't know why,
Maybe it doesn't feel right.
Maybe it feels right,
To walk away.
Yet, I feel bad,
I feel sad,
It feels like I lost you,
When I finally had my chance.
It was my chance,
And again, I walked away.
Why do I repeat the mistake?
Maybe it's not a mistake.
Maybe I'm right,
Maybe I'm wrong,
Either way,
So long…

MY ANGEL

Soft spoken, the voice of an angel,
Music to my ears,
A soothing sound,
No more fears.
She's my guardian,
She watched over me,
I was in prison,
But she set me free.

I owe her my life,
But she wants nothing in return,
I'm in hell,
But I will never burn,
Because she is an angel,
Who watched over me,
I was in prison,
But she has set me free.

She wants nothing more,
Than to watch over me,
She is my guardian angel,
She has set me free…

(…To her, I am the only thing that matters…)

(…I am her life…)

I MIGHT TELL YOU

I might tell you, what's in my heart,
once and for all, because
it might be the last thing I do,
before I fall.

But what if I tell you,
and it causes me to fall more,
and I end up worse off, than I was before?

Are some things better left unsaid,
should I stay strategic,
playing games with your head?

But do you think of me,
when I am not around?

Do you feel lost, but with me,
you're found?

Or do you just feel lost?

Is it hopeless?
Am I worth it?
What's my purpose?
I'm not perfect.
Not for you,
but I will be,
for somebody.

Somebody is out there for me.

IT HIT ME

…Like a train, it hit me,
I have to stay in this place for a while,
I must not move on too quickly,
I must enjoy the things around me,
I must enjoy this period of my life…

WHY I AM ALONE

And I wonder why I am alone,
Why I never let anyone in,
There is no girl in my life,
Because I never put the effort in.

When a girl does enter my life,
I seem to push them away,
Not because I do something wrong,
I never give them a reason to stay.

I never tell them how I feel,
And so they never feel appreciated.
They feel like I don't care,
They feel like they are hated.

And yet I don't know why,
I don't tell them what's in my heart,
Instead I let them walk away,
And each time it tears me apart.

It is never their fault,
I am always to blame,
They tell me they love me,
But I never tell them I feel the same.

And so I wonder why I am alone,
Why I never let anyone in,
There is no girl in my life,
Because I never put the effort in.

FORGIVE THEM FATHER

Forgive them Father,
For they don't know what they do,
They go on causing pain,
And they will not listen to you.

They ruin their own lives,
And then they have the nerve to ask you why,
Seeing how selfish they can be,
Makes me want to cry.

They cause so much hurt,
How can you forgive them,
They do it over and again,
How many chances will you give them?

It's the ones who never let you down,
Who often feel alone,
Why are good people faced with pain,
Why haven't they reaped what they have sown?

They should get the best of what you have to offer,
To me, that seems fair,
I hate to say it,
But sometimes it doesn't seem like you care.

I guess you have your ways,
You know what's best for the entire globe,
I must accept the suffering,
Just like the book of Job.

I'M FREE

The whisper through the trees—reaches me.
The wisdom of the air—teaches me.
My life flashes before me—memory after memory.
My life is escaping me—last breath is taking me.
It has broken me.
The spirits are free, forgive me, free.
Wasted away—my life has been taken—away.
I fight to stay awake, what are the trees
whispering, what are they trying to take?
They tell me—something like—the air
will set you free—you will no longer
have to breathe—no more memory—
it teaches me—it reaches me—free.
Forgive me—I'm free.
Forgive me…
I'm free…

(…The Flaming Forest of a Figurative Past Forever Follows Me Around…)

WHAT CHANGED?

I never thought she would leave me,
No, I never thought she would leave me,
I thought maybe she would teach me,
What it takes to believe.

I never thought I'd see the day,
That she took everything with her,
Now I'm here left to stay,
Holding on to this picture.

Look at the smile on your face,
Why so happy then?
This memory I cannot erase,
What happened to us, Jenn?

What changed,
I still feel the same,
I loved you then,
And I love you today,
What changed?

CONFESS

She looks at the moon and says,
"I have something to confess,
right now my life's a mess,"
and then she begins to take off her dress.

I WAS A CURSE

…I took my time to look,
To study this situation,
I didn't know what to expect,
I didn't know what I was facing.
How can something so simple,
Turn out to be unexpected,
I've never felt so lost,
I've never felt so neglected.
How did it come to this,
Was it really that bad,
Did I turn everything to dust,
How can it be so sad?
I didn't really know this,
But at that specific time,
I thought I was doing good,
I thought things would turn out fine.
I didn't know I screwed our lives up,
I didn't know I made things worse,
I guess me being around,
Was all just a curse…

THE NEXT TIME

The next time I have the chance,
I am going to say that I love you,
I'm no longer afraid,
I'm going to tell you I feel for you.
I'm not going to let anyone else have you,
Like I've already done,
I will not let you go,
I'm not going to run.
This time it will be different,
I will give it my best,
And if it doesn't work out,
At least I know I did my best.

BEAUTIFUL SILENCE

beautiful silence
silence is beautiful
so respected
i feel your soul
your eyes are truth
so beautiful
so blue
the eyes of you
are so beautiful
i don't need to speak
either do you
this silence
is so true
so beautiful
so amazing
so everlasting
so true
so beautiful
your soul
you
true
you

SO MUCH TO SAY

…Let it be, let it go,
Maybe they don't need to know,
Maybe they don't want me to know,
Sometimes the truth hurts,
Sometimes the truth makes it worse.
So let it be, let it go…

YOU WILL ALWAYS BE ALONE

I think you need to take a step back,
Take a look at your entire life,
Then you will see what I see,
You will see why we are right.

We want the best for you,
We don't want your life to slip you by,
We don't want you to wake up one day,
And wonder, yeah, wonder why.

You are repeating the same mistakes,
You are on the same path,
You will be dependent on the first person that comes along,
And for this reason it will fail to last.

And so you work so hard,
In order to distract yourself,
We just want you to come home,
Cause we are all here to help.

It's time to go for what you want,
And not the first thing that comes along,
At first it will be hard,
But you just have to be strong.

Sometimes you just have to listen,
To what others have to say,
Sometimes you need a little help,
So you can find your own way.

And if you choose to stay there,
Even if you are not on your own,
Even if you keep yourself busy,
You will always feel alone.

LOVE DANCE

This is where the truth comes to die,
It will make her smile, and it will make her cry.
It won't be a fairytale, it will be real,
It won't be make believe, it will be something she can feel.
It will linger in her heart, but it won't stay there forever,
It will tear it apart, and it won't put it back together.

It's the best of both worlds, it's the best feeling
She has ever had,
The something that can put a smile on her face,
Can also make her sad.
And it all comes down to a matter of chance,
Will she partake in this love dance?
Will she partake in this love dance?

COMFORTABLY NUMB

…I wonder if the day will come,
where I become,
comfortably numb, forever.

It will creep in like a curse,
and the worst,
at first, will get better.

And then I'll hit the state,
where nothing is great,
but fate, will bring it together…

MAYBE I AM HAPPY

Maybe I am happy, maybe this is all there is.
If I can overcome anything, why should I be scared?
Maybe I wasn't thinking clearly, maybe now I am?
I have this feeling, as if everything is going according
to plan. I'm not afraid anymore, I'm really not.
It didn't turn out the way I thought, but that's ok.
If I never share a connection with anyone in this life
again, that is fine, as long as I can keep my thoughts,
as long as I can keep my mind. They say that it is better
to have loved and lost than not have loved at all,
I say I would rather be me, than change
my life for someone. If I can remain real and still
feel alive, then I shall live, the day I become someone
else is the day I die. I will never, never live a lie.
I am not here to please everybody and not everybody
is here to please me, I understand this now. We
have our differences, we all change, nothing remains
the same. But if we are to change, we must remain true,
we must remain true to ourselves.
I may suffer on my own a lot in this life, but that's the price
of freedom. I know one day I will be free, and I will find you,
you, the girl who loves me for me. I know I will be surrounded
by people who look up to me, because I will have become the
person they wish they could be. I know this will happen
someday, but I still don't know how, but I know when it
happens, I will able to say, "Just look at me now."

SUPPOSED TO BE

…So far from you,
I'm right where I'm supposed to be,
Right beside you,
Just wasn't right for me…

THE PRISON OF MY MIND

It is all locked inside,
The prison of my mind.
And no one has the key,
Except me.

I'm afraid to set them free,
Because I don't know how it will be,
On the outside,
They feel safe inside.

They have accepted their fate,
They have never tried to escape,
They take comfort in doing time,
Inside my mind.

Yet, one day they will be released,
They will fill up thousands of sheets,
From prison to the top of the charts,
From my mind to their hearts.

(...From the prison of my mind to the freedom of their hearts...)

ONE DAY

And…
　　　…One day I will no longer be around,
　　I may be far away, I may be in the ground.
　　　It doesn't matter where I have gone,
　　But what matters is that I will be gone.
　　　　All I will be is a memory,
　　　And life will go on without me…

　　　(…And life will go on with me…)

IT'S TOO LATE

And now that you are gone,
I feel feelings of depression coming on.
I know I can stay strong,
But I don't know for how long.

And now I see the wisdom in you leaving,
Until you were gone, I did not know what I was feeling.
A long time ago I should have conceded,
And let you know that you were needed.

And now I know that I need you,
But I don't know what this will lead to.
I'm afraid you might be too far away,
And I'm too ashamed to pray.

And now I realize I must let you go,
I must suppress what I now know.
I must believe we were not meant to be,
And pray you have a good life without me.

(…And when I'm gone maybe then you'll see, what this life will be like after me…)

(…Without you…without me…)

SOME DAYS

Some days I just want to write,
And tell the world how I feel inside.
Share with them all that I am,
And all the things I try to hide.

If I did, would they listen,
Or would they pretend not to hear,
Would they leave me out in the cold,
And wait for me to disappear?

Some days I just want to sing,
And make the world hear my voice,
Make them listen to every word,
As if they never had a choice.

If I did, would it make a difference,
Would others actually follow my lead,
Gain the courage to make a change,
And help all of those in need?

Some days I want to change the world,
But I just never knew how,
But I know if I write and sing,
I can make a difference now.

YOU WILL SEE

They say I'm good for nothing,
So I'm going to prove them wrong,
Take everything I've learned,
And turn my life into a song.
I'll take that song to the edge of the world,
For everyone to hear,
Touch all of your hearts,
These words, you'll hold dear.
A nobody becomes somebody,
But I haven't changed.
But now they love me,
Even though I'm still the same.
They all want to know me,
Just another price of fame,
They pretend to be my friend,
Because they all know my name.
It doesn't seem fair does it,
I can't say I love it,
I'll fight my way through it,
And one day I'll rise above it.
I'll be in a position to make a difference,
To make strides,
Make this world a better place,
And change lives.
Metaphorically take my hand,
And I will lead you there,
If you ask me why,
Know that, it's because I care.
You can count on me,
I will never let you down,
Whenever you need me,

I will always be around.
I am the man I say I am,
And I always will be,
I hope you know I ran,
Because you looked down on me.
Even though I will never forgive you,
Because of you, I made my life better,
They said I'm good for nothing,
There's not a day I don't remember.
It motivates me to work hard,
To give it my all.
And in spite of you,
I will make sure I never fall.
I'm motivated by hatred,
You will love the person I can be,
You will realize I was great all along,
One day you will see…

(…One day they will see what their criticism has done to me…)

TO MY GRANDPA

I have seen a man, some 70 years old,
He stepped out into the light, and began to tell a story never told.
With the six string playing the tune, they all hung on every word,
After he was done, he walked away like nothing occurred.
But everyone who heard him sing, will never be the same,
Everyone who heard him sing, has changed.
He inspired the uninspired, with that simple song,
He gave life to the dead, he made the weak turn strong.
He was the voice of the wise, a man who never aged,
Anyone who has heard him sing, is saved.
And the older he gets, the better he plays,
Appreciate the once unappreciated, now amazed.
And I once was lost, but now I am found,
With your amazing grace, you will always be around.

THIS IS NOT MY LIFE

I have worked so hard, and for what,
To be discontent? To feel like I'm stuck?
I have been living this life, but it isn't mine,
I've done what they told me to do, and now I'm behind.
I feel as if I should start over, but I don't know how,
I feel like I'm trapped, and I feel like it is too late now.
I will never be able to live my own life, I watch it waste away,
The longer I let this go on, is just another wasted day.
I wish I had the courage to escape, to love my own life,
To be free every day, and be free every night.
To live my life to the fullest, with no regrets,
To know I always gave it my all, to know that I did my best.
I want to run away from this life, because it isn't me,
I want to get away from this prison, I want to be free.

(…I want to break free…)

BRING A PERSON DOWN

There are so many things, that can bring a person down,
So many reasons for depression, you just have to look around.
It's a crazy world we live in, this I say is true,
But it all depends, on how you let it affect you.
Yeah, some people are depressed, they let it hurt,
All those horrible things they see, make them feel like dirt.
Often they think too much, to the point they actually feel,
Some things might not even exist, but to them it's real.
They become a victim, a victim of their own mind,
They fall into a slippery slope of pain, pain they try to find.
Once they are down, they feel like they won't be up again,
They often feel trapped, they often feel like it's the end.
But only if they saw the good around them, only if that became their focus,
Then maybe they would see, that they are not hopeless.
That there is good in this world, they just have to see it,
Make it a part of their life, and actually believe it,
They can be happy, they just have to choose to be.
It's true, but at first it did seem like news to me,
I was trapped in misery, he was the only friend to me,
But it is my life, I choose what to see.
I just want you to listen, because this can change your life,
It's all in your hands, it's time to make things right.

SOUL MATE

When I think about it,
I can remember you but nothing else,
Not the things I've done,
Or the way I felt.

I lost it all along the way,
Time made everything disappear,
It cleared up my mind,
And got me thinking clear.

It's hard to feel grateful,
Because it seems like it was good just the other day,
And I will only let it go,
Once I have nothing more to say.

This could take a year,
Or maybe even ten,
I know I have to quit thinking of you,
For it to all end.

But how can I forget about you,
If you have changed my life?
You took the worst possible things,
And you made me see the light.

I never got the chance to thank you,
Because I never knew how,
I think I finally figured it out,
But it's too late now.

So I dedicate this to you,
Knowing you will never see it,
But I wrote it with false hope,
That maybe someday you will read it.

(…The more I write about you,
The longer you remain in my mind,
As I do this I finally realize,
My writing is the only thing that keeps the thought of you alive.

If I give up writing about you,
It would feel like I would be losing you twice,
Honestly writing about you,
Has been a big part of my life.

You mean more to me today in my writing,
Than you did in my past,
It's only through writing,
That you will continue to last.

But I'm taking all the good from you,
And forgetting about the bad,
All I'm doing is creating a girl,
That I wish I had…)

SLEEPLESS NIGHTS

Can sleepless nights
create a life
out of thin air
with others
unaware?

Can words breathe
come alive
and give meaning
to our
being?

Can what I create
at night
change my life
once people
hear?

I think it's clear
that sleep
means dreams
nothing is as
it seems?

If I slept
nothing would exist
this life
would not be born
at night.

(...If I slept
I would dream.
The dream,
I dream
would disappear,
once my eyes
open. Nothing
would survive
the night. But
if I stay up
and write, I
can create and
give life at
night. Something
that now exists
would not have
existed. To produce
you have to be
gifted, to be gifted
you have to use
it. To sleep, means
your gift is
wasted, to dream,
while the morning
erased it.
I give life to
the words I
write at
night...)

BLACK

How can a man who hurts so deeply, hide is so discreetly,
and for so long? He must be eating up inside, soon he will
no longer be able to hide. Everything will go wrong all
at once, and it won't stop, until he hits rock bottom. Black.
And I was the one who brought him back.
And I was the one who brought him back…

…That's what I like to tell myself…

But it was a long road, he made his choice,
and I wasn't afraid, I used my voice.
I wrote him letters, hoping he would get better,
this I repeated, hoping he would remember.
I told him to never give up not matter what happens, life's a
choice, so choose,
but if you keep doing what you're doing, you're going to
lose.
Yeah, life's a choice, I taught him that,
and when he hit rock bottom, Black,
I brought him back.
Yeah, I was the one who brought him back…

… That's what I like to tell myself…

(…I saved a life…)

I SEE HELL

You want to know the truth?
Hell is all around us,
We see it every day.

Now some people,
They choose to ignore it,
And it doesn't get in their way.

Others are trapped,
They care about the world,
And for this they pay.

I can't ignore it,
I see parts of hell around me,
I know this is not okay.

I want to change it,
I will change it,
That is all I have to say.

(…What really matters?…)

MAKE YOUR MARK

Go out in the world one day and make your mark,
Give it your all, and touch their heart.
Just one day, that's all you have to live for,
And after that day, you will become so much more.
Do it now before it is too late,
Before it slips you by, before you fill with hate.
Another day, is another day gone by,
It's time to show them, it's time you try.
Don't worry, and if you fall,
Well, I guess it wasn't meant to be after all.

UNKNOWN

Why would someone want to be so alone,
Why does he push everyone away,
Why does he try to escape,
And wonder why they never stay?

What is he afraid of?
I don't think he really knows,
He says that he wants you to forget him,
Yet, he doesn't want to be alone.

It seems like he wants to fall,
And lose everything he has,
He doesn't want anything,
But yet he is always sad.

Even the ones he loves,
They don't seem to care,
They never ask if he is okay,
Maybe they are just unaware?

It could be that he likes to hide,
No one knows what he is about,
They think he must be doing fine,
There is simply nothing to figure out.

But, the truth is, he is hurting inside,
He wishes someone could understand,
Simply get to know him,
Simply know who I am.

TOO NORMAL

...I think I'm just too normal and that's my problem...too smart for my own good...I wish maybe that I was a little crazy...just like everyone else...

KEEP ME HOME

For years now I've been telling myself and everyone else that I want to go away…but the truth is I just want someone to tell me that they want me to stay…I want you to know, I need someone to be the reason to keep me here, and if no one comes along before it's time to go, that has always been my biggest fear. And if I must go, I'm afraid I will end up alone, in a place I do not know.

I don't want to be alone,
I want you to keep me home,
But I guess I'm on my way…
I just want someone to tell me
That they want me to stay…
Don't you want me to stay.
Please tell me you want me to stay.
I don't want to go away.
Please tell me you want me to stay.

BEAUTY OF YOUR LIFE

...I want to be a part of the beauty of your life,
I don't want to sit alone, again on another cold night.

She won't let me into her world, I'm left behind.

I'm good at running, leaving you alone, I wish I always had you...

SOLITUDE

The light of solitude,
I speak of the weight,
The lack of burden,
Positivity.

One must look for it,
Search in the situation,
How can I feel peace,
Right now.

No one to let down,
The light of solitude,
Nothing to prove,
Nothing to
Lose.

Freedom for one,
Depressing for others,
But do not judge,
What you don't know,
Solitude for one,
Is
Freedom
For
Some…

(… Maybe I've been alone so long that it no longer seems wrong…)

MY WORLD TURNED

The day I realized my dreams died,
all I did was go numb, I never cried.
A part of my life ended, on that one single day,
my whole world turned, everything I knew slipped away.
I was left all by myself, no one stuck around,
no one was there to pick me up, when I was down.
I had to reevaluate my whole life, and create new dreams,
a new beginning, is not as simple as it seems.
Especially when you loved your old life, you never wanted
to see it go,
but you watched it all disappear, everything you know.
And your new life,
will never be as good as your old life could have been,
and it feels like you will forever lose and never win.
But yet, you have to make the most out of it, somehow,
and you know you will never feel worse, than you do now.
In a way, you know, that it can only get better.
But still it is tough, to keep it all together.
Sometimes you feel like giving up, sometimes it doesn't
seem worth it, sometimes if feels hopeless,
and sometimes you feel worthless.
But you keep going, even if you don't know why,
something deep down, wants you to try.
And so you give it your all, you accept who you are,
even if you fell, you will always be a star.

(...I realized I will never be the person I always wanted to
be. I had to accept this, or I have to accept this, because
honestly, I haven't yet...)

EXIST

…I want to enter their life,
I want them to know I exist.
I want to make a difference,
I want to be missed.

I no longer want to sit back,
I've been doing this for too long,
I want to give it my all,
I want to be strong.

I want them to know the truth,
I want them to know what is in my heart,
If I keep it all inside,
It will tear me apart.

I've been afraid for years,
But I don't want to be anymore,
I want them to notice me,
I want to be so much more.

And I can be,
I just have to try,
But for some reason I can't,
And I don't know why.

I just want to enter their life,
I want them to know I exist,
I want to make a difference,
I want to be missed…

(…I'm in conflict with my own self: I want to be forgotten, I don't want to be forgotten; I want to be known, I don't want to be known. I want to be trapped in oblivion, yet, I want them to hold on to me forever, and keep the thought of me alive. I want to be immortal in the minds of others, in the lives of others. Through other people I will never die, but without other people I will never be alive…)

ME AGAINST THE WORLD

Maybe I do feel unstoppable,
Maybe I can do what I want,
What does it matter to you?
You never cared before.

Now that my life is getting better,
Now you want to get involved,
Where were you when I was down,
Why do you come around now?

You make me feel worse,
I hate the show you put on,
I know what you are trying to do,
You're like a double sided mirror.
(I see right through you)

But what if I fall again,
Will you disappear?
Will I struggle on my own,
Will I face the whole world again?

Or will I escape,
This time for good,
Or will you stick around,
Or will I just not fall again?

(…When I'm left alone to face the world again,
It's just me against the world, no one is on my side, I am my own pride…)

TO MY BROTHER

You leave my world, and I, can't turn things back,
to how they used to be, and I, no longer
know you, and you no longer know me.
And we can't turn things back,
No…

But we must move on, yeah, we must move on.

Remember how I used to look up to you,
And follow you around?
And you used to cheer me up,
When I was feeling down.
But where are you now?
Thousands of miles away, you moved away.
Yeah, you moved away.

You leave my world, and I, can't turn things back,
to how they used to be, and I, no longer
know you, and you no longer know me.
And we can't turn things back,

No…we can't turn things back.

But we must move on, yeah, we must move on.

So far away, and a lifetime ago,
so many things we no longer know.
It seems so different now, so much has changed,
and I don't know how.

And I love to look back on how it used to be,
because you were always there for me, and I hold on,
but it's all gone.

You leave my world, and I, can't turn things back,
to how they used to be, and I, no longer
know you, and you no longer know me,
And we can't turn things back,

No…we can't turn things back.

But we must move on, yeah, we must move on…

THAT'S WHY THEY HATE ME

I step outside late at night,
For a walk around the block,
To clear my mind,
To get these thought to stop.
So much going on lately,
I wonder why they hate me.
I've done nothing wrong.
I've been singing the same ol'song.
But yet they fail to understand,
It's just a part of who I am.

They cannot change me,
And that's why they hate me,
Yeah, that's why they hate me.

Why do they put the effort in,
Over and over again,
Why do they care?
Why are they not aware,
That this is who I am?
And this is who I will always be,
Why can they not see?

That they cannot change me,
And that's why they hate me,
Yeah, that's why they hate me.

And when I returned home,
I was on my own,
They must have gone,
Maybe they moved on.

Can I blame them?
Now they understand,
This is who I am.

And that's why they cannot change me,
And that's why they hate me.
Yeah, that's why they hate me…

JUST A MEMORY

He's out in the cold,
A man of old,
They asked him to stay,
But he hopped on a train,

And said, "Take me away
I want to erase,
The memories of this place.
I've seen it all…"

And the last boarding call,
Let him know, that soon he would be free,
Just a memory, yeah, just a memory.

And the steel train tracks,
Helped him relax,
Just like they always did,
And he felt like a kid.

Once again,
He was a drifter, an old friend.
And soon he would be free,
Just a memory, yeah, just a memory.

And he sat alone,
Leaving his home, behind,
And his life flashed by,
In his mind.

Everything he loved,
Everything he was seeing,

Was everything he was leaving,

And he thought, "Why am I leaving,
What am I hoping to see? I will never be free, I will be,
Just a memory, yeah, just a memory."

That man of old was me,
And I am just a memory.

DEATH DEFIER

And he calls them his friend,
the walls are talking to him again.
And the phone rings, but there is no one,
on the other end.
What the fuck is happening to him?
Is he losing his mind, leaving sanity
behind? It all changes in a minute,
what is real and what isn't,
paranoid schizophrenia, drug induced
dementia, is taking over his life,
all day and all night.
He's trapped in a hell, how many
stories will he tell? We know he is lying,
and he feels like he is flying, but
inside he is dying, while his family
is crying. A heartless darkness has taken
over, no longer sober, mental disorder,
caused by a choice, and the voice,
yeah the voice, says end it all, once
and for all. No one wants to see you
fall, these choices are hating, leading and
persuading. He just wants them to stop,
he hits bottom like a rock. And the
phones rings, this time someone is on the
other end, a friend, a true friend.

It's time to put an end to it all, and
bring you back to life,
it's time to make things right,
and fight the good fight.
It's time to come back home,

cause you are not alone,
it's time to come back to
life, that voice saved his life.
And he was put to the ultimate
test, and he defied death.
Now that life is better, all
he can do is remember, is that
he changed forever.

STAGE FRIGHT

The sunlight is blinding me,
but I'm inside,
spotlight, stage fright,
where's that bug I catch,
the one that will lead to
stardom, greatness,
immortality?

(…A legend in their eyes…)

THE HISTORIES

Magnificent and triumphant,
For the sake of wisdom.
The earth sings,
Beauty and warmth,
Overcoming shadows.

Thee who speaks to be heard,
Falls beneath the sound,
Oblivion in the forest,
Lost amongst the waves.

Fortune has been told,
For thousands of years,
Only turtles and stones,
Have witnessed it all.
All knowing.

The life of cycles,
Has one ultimate truth,
The ancients feared it,
Others didn't listen,
When the truth was told.

A standstill of time,
But continuously moving on.
Evolution is living,
Triumphant, forever…

(…Prophecies of a madman will never be acknowledged until you make them come true…remember that…)

A MILLION DIFFERENT WAYS

…What it all comes down to,
Life can go a million different ways…

THE LOST LONELY STRANGER

…Why do people stare,
        When you walk down the road?

Yet, they turn away,
    When you're carrying such a…heavy load.

And they want you to go back,
        To where the river flowed.

    Lost lonely stranger,
            Man with no name,
Go back to where you…came.
    Lost lonely stranger,
            All eyes are on you,
      It's time to move on through…

You're not welcome here.
You're not welcome here.
        No you're not welcome here,
    Not welcome here.

    It's time you leave,
    This old desert town,
No one here wants you around,
    Lost lonely stranger,
      You,
    Lost Lonely Stranger…

THE DOORS

Have you entered those Doors
of perception,
infinite, immaculate?

Where the "People are strange"
and Mr. Mojo Risin',
rises, and falls,
and reaches "The End,"
but yet remains infinite,
locked inside the doors
of perception?

Have you heard him sing,
the man known as
The Lizard King?
It's like entering a dream,
a new reality, yet
when one awakens, he
awakens only to
scream.
And all the doors
of perception,
remain forever
locked
behind him.

THE BOTTLE

I think about hitting the bottle,
And letting another night spill into 2morrow.
Bring on the sorrow,
And let me quarrel
With myself,
Some say I need help,
I say I have it all under control,
They say I'm at an all-time low,
What do they know?
I know I'm in control,
The bottle doesn't control me,
It sobers me, it helps me see,
The person I can be.
Yeah, it's the whiskey
That frees me from
Suffocations, from obligations,
From all those fearful situations.
It's the bottle that helps me
See 2morrow.

AM I DREAMING?

Maybe I'm not awake,
Maybe this is a dream,
Maybe that is why I feel numb.
I'm just living in a scene,
But I can't feel anything.

Life just passes me by,
And it's like I don't care,
It doesn't feel real,
So why should it matter?
Do I try to awake myself?

Or do I wait 'till I'm fully rested,
Or for my alarm clock to go off?
If this is a dream,
What is being awake like?
Is it something to be desired?

What if we are all sleeping,
And we awake when we die?
Everyone dies, therefore,
Everyone will be awaken.
That's something to take comfort in.

Either way, I don't plan to awaken soon,
And I don't plan to die.
But I do plan to feel this dream, (To make the most of it)
To remember this dream,
Because it might be all I have…

(…Maybe life is just a dream…)

SO REFINED

*...I'm afraid of that my ability to hide
will result in me becoming so refined,
that I am no longer me...*

MAN WHO WRITES

...I'm starting to see a large difference between the man that writes and the man that lives...I have become a walking contradiction...

...But maybe that's why a lot of writers are depressed, they can't possibly live up to the things they write about, they can't follow their own advice. Maybe the ones who are successful, accept and understand this fact...

...In a way we are all walking contradictions at one point or another, from one situation to the other...

...Freedom is being myself, and yet I'm afraid to be free... It just doesn't make sense does it?...

...I think that in this day and age just simply being yourself is one of the hardest things to do...

...Is it possible to just be yourself without others looking down on you, even though you're the one who is sane, you're the one who is true?...

...Society teaches us to hide, how to not be ourselves, and how to become someone else...

TRUTH

…I've got cold feet,
literally, I have bare feet
and I'm standing on concrete.
That's the truth,
there is no secret meaning,
and I'm not speaking metaphorically.
I want to tell the truth for once.
Does poetry always have to be a lie?
Do words always have to have a double meaning?
Why can't the sky just be blue, the sun
hot, and water wet?
Is that not poetry?
Is that not beauty?
It is the truth,
and sometimes, that's
all that matters…

UNSURE

Grown men look at me,
As if I have all the answers,
While everyone is unsure,
They assume that I know what to do.
Maybe they look at me,
Because they trust me,
Because I am always there,
Because I'm calm in all situations.

The hardest thing for me,
Is to take control when they look to me,
They expect so much,
That I become unsure.
I just don't want to let others down,
I don't want to fail them.
But the truth is, what do I know?
I am 22 years old,
Why would they look to me?

Is it possible that I do know more than them?
That I do have the answers,
That I can make the right decision,
That I am wise beyond my years?
I see the dangers of this,
I see the pressure,
But it is my chance to do good,
Whereas some do not get that chance.

A TEAR FALLS

A tear falls and makes its mark,
It's a little piece of my heart.
A piece that I will leave behind,
A piece I will never find.

A tear falls and stains the page,
It will always remain even when I change.
A tear that falls in this book,
Will probably be overlooked.

That piece of my heart will always be here,
But no one can see an invisible tear.
In a sense it is a hidden treasure,
Never found, but it will be here forever.

Only I will know it is here,
And the average reader won't really care.
That tear might be tough to see,
But they will be reading a part of me.

A tear falls and makes its mark,
It's a little piece of my heart.
A piece that I will leave behind,
A piece I will never find.

STRIVE FOR

I need someone to love,
Someone to strive for,
Someone to die and cry for.
Someone to try for,
Someone to hold my head up high for.

Someone to fall for,
Someone to give my all for.
Someone to call for,
Someone to stand tall for.
Someone to let this wall down for.

I see it now,
I just need a girl to strive for.

(…And the rest will follow…)

ONE DAY

It's 4am, she's thinking of him
Why did he have to leave?
Why did she believe,
That he would stay,
When she's the one that pushed him…away?
She didn't want him to break her heart,
So she decided to drift apart.
She slowly let him fade away,
She gave him no reason to stay.

And one day he was gone,
One day he moved on,
And she realized she was wrong,
And she needed him all along,
And one day he was gone.
And now it was too late,
She chose her own fate
And he was gone…

She walked to the window,
Time moved by slow,
While she looked outside,
The tears fell from her eyes,
She will always be alone,
Her heart turns to stone,
She will never love again,
Yet, she was the reason it had to end.

And one day he was gone,
One day he moved on,
And she realized she was wrong,

And she needed him all along,
And one day he was gone.
And now it was too late,
She chose her own fate
And he was gone…

LIKE A STRANGER

…I've been living my life like a stranger,
Even though I'm living in my home town,
No one really knows me,
Yet, I've always been around…

HER ADVICE

…She said, "Why don't you leave this place,
If no one knows who you are,
Why stay trapped here,
If you can go out and be a star?"

I took that advice,
And made it my life,
I moved away,
Far, far away.

One day I will be back,
And I'll say look at me now,
And everyone that looked down on me,
Will simply wonder, how?

I will become greater than life,
Greater than they could ever be,
One day I will show them,
Yeah, one day they will see…

INTROSPECTION

...Here's a life lesson, try introspection,
Learn about integrity, and about your identity.
Become your biggest fan, become your own man,
Learn from your mistakes, learn how to be great.
Be true, be you, do all you can do.
Never settle for less, always be your best,
Take everything in stride, never run and hide.
Always be open, always flow like the ocean...

SHE WILL SEE

...Even though things seem improbable,
Nights like this make me feel unstoppable.
I finally feel better than everyone else,
And I finally feel like I can be myself.
The truth is I know more than others do,
Yeah, you heard me, I know more than you.
One day we will come together,
Even if I have to wait forever,
I can see in your eyes,
That one day you will realize,
That I am right,
But tonight is not that night.
We've got months, even years to live,
But no one will be able to give what I can give,
One day you will see,
One day you will notice me...

I'M FALLING

…I'm falling,
Forgive me now,
I know I am too late,
But just hear me out.

I need you,
I always have,
But I was afraid,
To be myself.

Never good enough,
That's how I felt,
I thought you deserved better,
But there is no one else.

I need you,
To trust me now,
To take my hand,
For this I vow:

I am the man,
That is right for you,
I would give everything,
Even my life for you.

I'm falling for you,
Forgive me now,
I waited too long,
But just hear me out…

MY PARADISE

...Far from here, an unknown paradise,
Is the place for me, to have a perfect life.
A place far from the cold, I will no longer be frozen,
I want to live in the sunshine, somewhere near the ocean.
Sand between the toes, and a warm breeze,
Seashells, and palm trees...

WHEN LIFE GOES WRONG

When rain turns to thunder,
When the sky turns black,
When it follows you around,
How do you stay on track?

When shit slides downhill,
When it all crashes into you,
When you feel you can't escape,
How do you make it through?

When everything is perfect,
When you are feeling strong,
When life is good,
Why does it go wrong?

(…When you're on track, it's easy to know where you are headed, and it's easier for the black clouds to follow you around…)

RELASPSE 2 RECOVERY

I must be changing, refraining, from simply rearranging,
I feel different, no longer inconsistent, but forever persistent.
I am better, forever, holding it together,
I'm giving thanks, and taking my strength to greater lengths.
I'm breaking out, and taking out, everything that gets in my way.
A new day, I pray, for God to show me the way,
A new insight to life, finally I see the light.
No longer slanted, no longer taking things for granted,
My life is not how I planned it, but I understand it,
And that's all that matters, my world turned, but it didn't shatter.
No longer stressed or depressed, in fact I feel like I'm at my best.

Relapse to recovery,
They can't expect much from me,
Covering the tracks,
To my relapse,
Leaving that all behind me,
Living day to day,
With God walking beside me.

My shoulders are back, my head is high, no pun intended,
For the first time. A chance to clear the air and my mind,
For the first time. Signing off on a new page, stepping on a new stage, thoughts are free, no longer caged, mind is clear no longer dazed, days no longer hazed.
I'm in a new phase, I've changed my ways,
I'm on a new path, and it feels like it's going to last…

Relapse to recovery,
They can't expect much from me,
Covering the tracks,
To my relapse,
Leaving that all behind me,
Living day to day,
With God walking beside me…

TIME FLIES BY

...Time flies by,
And so does a life
We need to slow things down,
Before it passes us by.
And all these good times
That we've had
They all stay locked
Inside the past...

THE SAD CLOWN

Everyone has heard of the Sad Clown,
The one who smiles, even when he is down.
Most people experience this in their life, but,
They don't know what living this way forever would be like.
It's a life they would never be able to imagine,
Let alone survive it if it actually happened.
The Sad Clown is a man of sacrifice,
He smiles so others can have a better life.

A REMINDER

...Just a reminder that sometimes you need to take a few steps back and look at the bigger picture in order to see what really matters in this life. Your blind to everything else when you're caught up on one thing...Remember that, and take a step back...

WISE OLD MAN

One day I was talking to an old man,
And he was looking back on his life.
And he said, "Son, let me give you some advice,
I've lived an odd 80 years,
And the best times I remember,
Are times I faced my fears.
And everything it led to,
Turned out to be the things that mattered most.
Like the time I packed my things,
And moved to the west coast,
That's where I met my wife,
And my family became my life.
What if I didn't move there?
But, Son, I faced my fears,
And I lived my life,
I moved away,
And met my wife,
I had three kids,
And raised them right.
Because I faced my fears,
I can sleep at night."

THE REALMS OF THE UNREAL (MY REALMS ARE REAL)

…He sits in his room alone, hiding from the world,
he has nothing to offer them, except what he writes
down on the pages, the pages he keeps to himself.
He does not know how to live, but he does know how to
hide. And when he dies, that's when he will come alive; when
they read how he felt inside.
It's sad to know that his genius will never be appreciated,
until it is too late. However, when one is alive he is seen as
insane, but when he is gone he is great. This irony causes him so
much pain, because he knows that he is the only one who is
sane, yet, so sane he is hated. Maybe not hated but unnoticed, he
is a ghost, he is unseen. But this man who is so alone, will be
greater than life someday. It's nights like this that make him
stronger, make him greater, and make him immortal. And so he
sits in his room alone, hiding from the world, so that one day
there will be a better tomorrow…

SACRIFICE

I never wanted to let you down,
But you don't know the things I've found,
They changed the way I chose to live,
I was meant to live selfless, I was meant to give.

I know it may not seem fair,
And I know it seems like I don't care.
The truth is I do not matter,
So that's why I let my dreams shatter.

I will let them strip me bare,
And they know I will always be there.
I need nothing in this life,
I am a sacrifice.

UNTIL YOU LET GO

Take my hand, and know,
You are mine, until you let go.
This is our moment,
Feel it, own it.
It's ours, forever,
It's ours, together.
No one can feel, how we feel,
Because what we have, is real.
What we have is true,
All that matters, is you.
So,
Take my hand, and know,
You are mine, until you let go…

MAYBE ONE DAY

…Maybe one day I will make a choice,
Find my voice, and stop living through Fitzgerald, Rand,
and Joyce…

THE PAST HAS PASSED

Maybe the past doesn't matter as much as I think it does,
So why am I trying to restore what once was?
Maybe it's ok for me to run,
And just forget all the things that I've done,
And forget all the people I once knew,
Maybe I need to forget you.

Maybe I need to lighten the load I carry around,
Maybe I need to choose a new road to go down.
Maybe I'm getting wise, maybe I'm getting older,
Maybe I'm just tired of carrying the weight of the world on my shoulders.
Maybe I'm just tired of trying to put the pieces together,
Maybe it's time for me to search for something better.

Maybe time does heal all wounds, maybe I'm healed,
Maybe I don't need to hide the wounds I've concealed.
Maybe I'm no longer afraid, maybe I am strong,
And maybe I'm finally ready to move on.
Maybe I will no longer wait for you to come back around,
Maybe the thought of you will no longer bring me down.

Maybe I will just forget the past,
And forget the things that failed to last.
Maybe I'll stop wishing that things would have turned out better,
Maybe I'll just stop trying to remember all together.
Maybe I'll stop wishing there was something more I could do,
And maybe, I'll just be happy for you…

About the Author

Jesse A. Murray is a Canadian author, poet, and high school teacher. He is most known for his debut novel *Love or Baseball?* (Released in 2018) and his debut poetry collection *I Will Never Break* (Released in 2020). Jesse is currently working on putting together a few more poetry collections from his early writings, and he is working on finishing his second novel, *Left On Base.*

Visit Jesseamurray.com for more information and current updates on Jesse's future projects.

www.ingramcontent.com/pod-product-compliance
Lightning Source LLC
Chambersburg PA
CBHW030917080526
44589CB00010B/353